Note to Learners

Welcome to Workbook 3! A book packed with fun activities to revi⬚
in books 1 and 2! As you work through this book, you may find t⬚ ⬚⬚⬚⬚⬚ ⬚ ⬚⬚ tricky. Don't
worry, you can have a look at pages 38-41 to remind you of what the words mean and look like!

As you work through this book, try to say the words out loud. The pronunciation of each word and the brush strokes for how to write them are available on our video tutorials—just go to www.superspeakjuniors.com or scan the QR code at the front of the book!

Enjoy learning to write one of the oldest languages in the world!

Note to Parents/Guardians

This workbook helps your child to revise the 200 words introduced to him/her in books 1 and 2 of our Beginners Chinese Writing Workbooks series. We do this by challenging their minds with fun activities so they can practise their Chinese writing and Chinese reading skills.

Ideally, your child will have worked through books 1 and 2. However, this is not necessary for them to work through this book as we have included all the vocabulary necessary on pages 38-41 in this book.

There is no need for you to have any knowledge of the Chinese language. The learner can view our free video tutorials "First 100 Chinese Words" and "Chinese Writing Workbook 2" on our website **www.superspeakjuniors.com**. In our tutorials we also demonstrate how to pronounce each word in **Cantonese** and in **Mandarin**, as well as how to write them.

Chinese can be written in a **Simplified** form and in a **Traditional** form. The Traditional form has more strokes and the Simplified form is simpler to write. We include both Simplified and Traditional Chinese characters within this book. Most of the words are the same in the Simplified and Traditional form. Where they differ, we have included both versions and will leave it up to you and your child to decide which version you wish to focus on.

We appreciate all children work differently and encourage they work at a pace suitable for them. Where possible, we suggest practising daily.

ISBN 978-1-8381799-60

All rights reserved. No part of this publication may be reproduced, stored or transmitted in any form or by any means, electronic, photocopying, recording or otherwise, without the prior written permission of the Publisher. Cover design and content produced by M Kan and H Wang.

New words not covered in Book 1 and Book 2:

Rat

鼠

syu2　shǔ

Tiger

虎

fu2　hǔ

Rabbit

兔

tou3　tù

Dragon

龍　龙

Traditional　Simplified

lung4　lóng

Snake

蛇

se4　shé

Monkey

猴

hau4　hóu

Chinese Zodiac Animals

In the Chinese lunar calendar, each year is named after an animal. Find your year of birth in the zodiac wheel to see which animal is your zodiac animal. Write it in Chinese below.

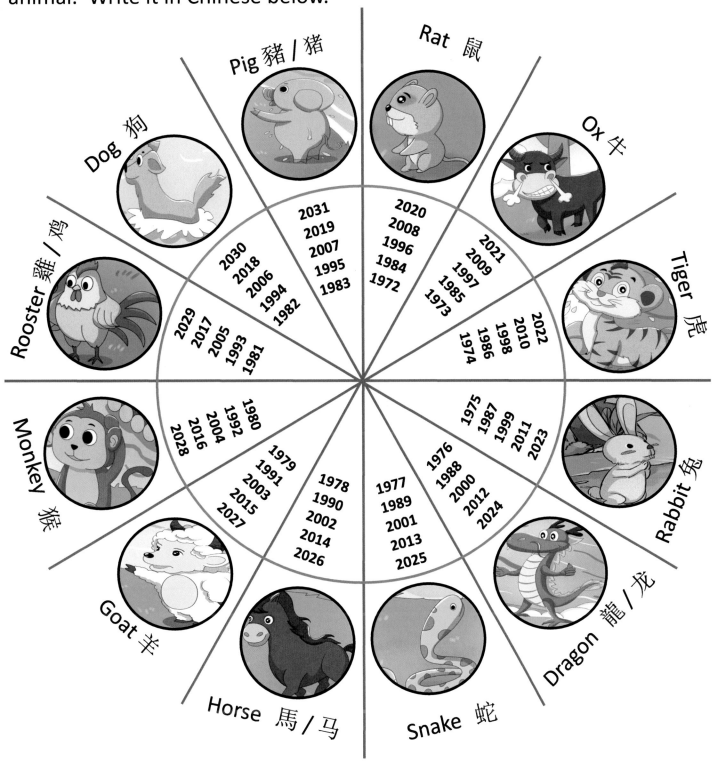

MY ZODIAC ANIMAL _____

How many?

Match the numbers below to the pictures.

一 二 三 四 五 六

Match It

Draw a line matching the Chinese word to the numeral.

一 ●   ● **1**

四 ●   ● **7**

三 ●   ● **2**

七 ●   ● **3**

十 ●   ● **9**

六 ●   ● **4**

九 ●   ● **10**

八 ●   ● **5**

二 ●   ● **8**

五 ●   ● **6**

Which is Correct?

Chinese words can look similar. Circle the correct word to match the picture.

a) 人　大

b) 口　田

c) 米　火

d) 木　禾

e) 日　目

f) 哥　歌

g) 女　安

h) 用　同

i) 王　玉

Match It

Draw a line matching the Chinese word to the correct picture.

子 ●   ●

和 ●   ●

美 ●   ●

到 ●   ●

面 ●   ●

在 ●   ●

Numbers

You know numbers 1 to 10 in Chinese. We will now show you how to say two digit numbers above 10 in Chinese.

Let's begin by talking about **place value**. Place value is the value of each digit in a number. Here are some examples:

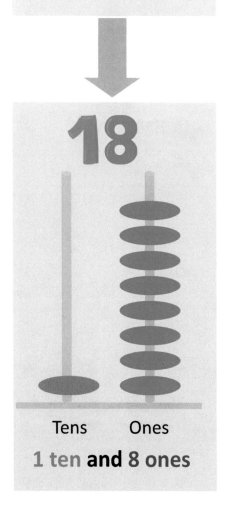

18

- Digit 1 represents 1 ten (or 10)
- Digit 8 represents 8 ones (or 8).

18

Tens   Ones

1 ten and 8 ones

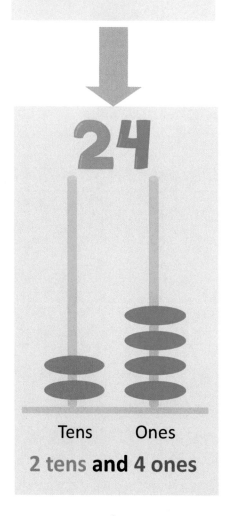

24

- Digit 2 represents 2 tens (20)
- Digit 4 represent 4 ones (or 4).

24

Tens   Ones

2 tens and 4 ones

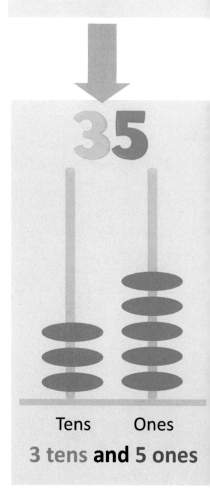

35

- Digit 3 represents 3 tens (or 30)
- Digit 5 represents 5 ones (or 5).

35

Tens   Ones

3 tens and 5 ones

We will now show you how to write the numbers in Chinese.

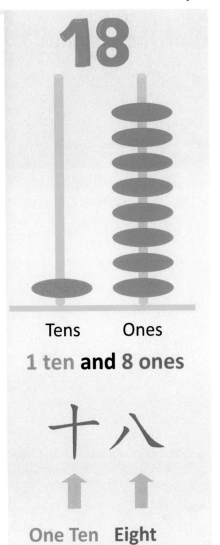

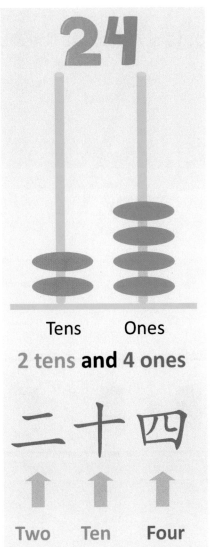

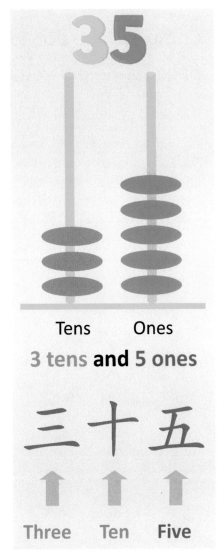

Here are some other numbers in Chinese:

11	十一	19	十九	27	二十七	35	三十五
12	十二	20	二十	28	二十八	36	三十六
13	十三	21	二十一	29	二十九	40	四十
14	十四	22	二十二	30	二十	50	五十
15	十五	23	二十三	31	三十一	60	六十
16	十六	24	二十四	32	三十二	70	七十
17	十七	25	二十五	33	三十三	80	八十
18	十八	26	二十六	34	三十四	90	九十

Dot-to-Dot

Complete the dot-to-dot below. Look at the numbers on the previous page for help if you need it.

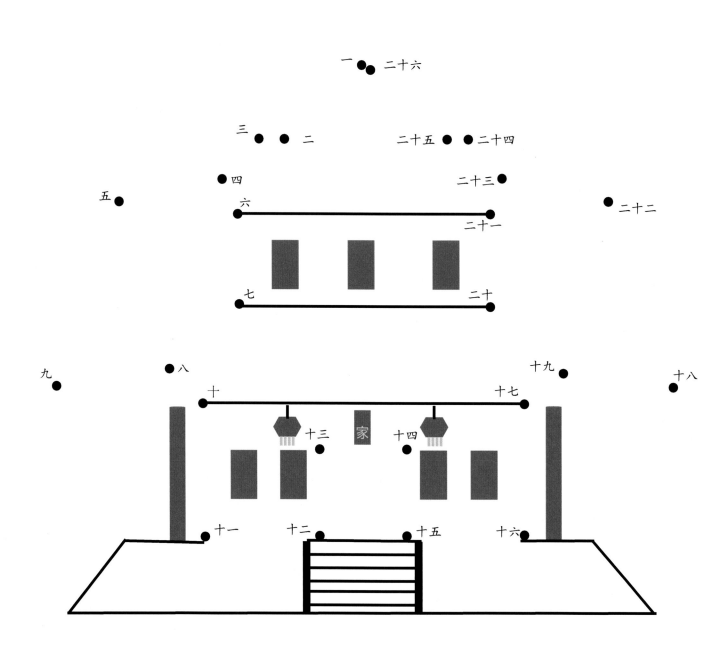

Draw The Animals

This farm is looking a bit empty. Draw the animals in the correct places!

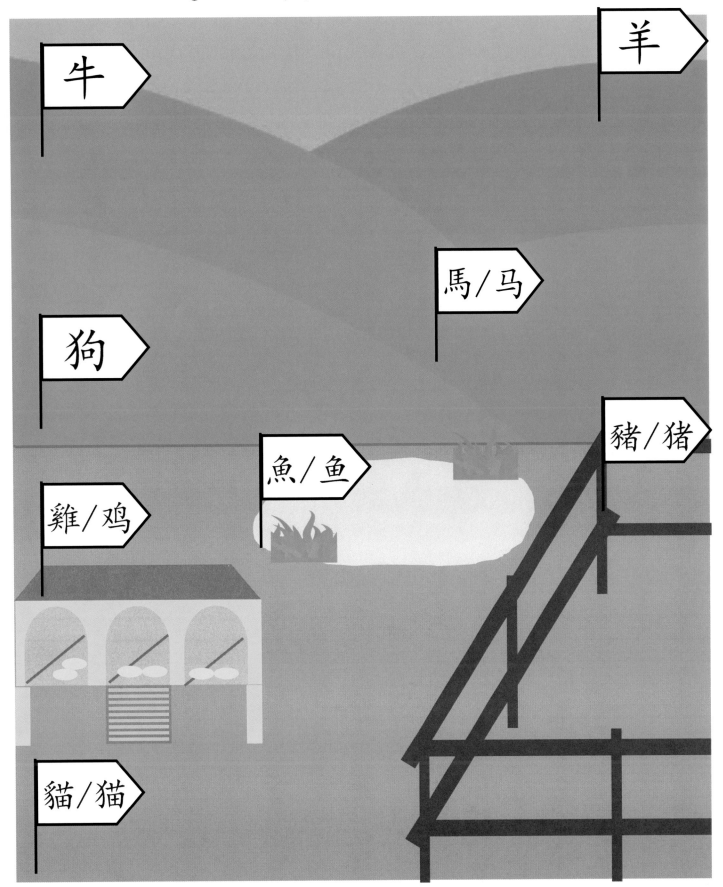

Make The Word

There is no alphabet in Chinese, but all Chinese words are made up of common parts. Some of these common parts are simple Chinese words. Some of these simpler words that frequently appear in other Chinese words are in the word bank below. See if you can combine the words in the blue box to make the correct Chinese word for each of the blank spaces. The first one has been done for you.

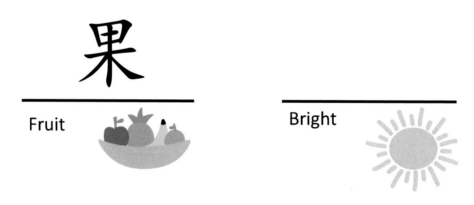

Fruit

Bright

Early

Ancient

Minute/ Divide

Sing

Male

Out

Translation

Pick a word from the top table and link it with a word from the bottom table to translate the English words below into Chinese. Write them on the blank lines below.

小	學/学	生	火	明
好	父	中	可	早

心	心	口	母	生
白	文	日	山	上

Careful _____

Kind _____

Parents _____

Chinese _____

Tasty _____

Morning _____

Student _____

Birthday _____

Volcano _____

Understand _____

Circle The Common Part

As we mentioned on the previous page, many Chinese words are made up of common parts. See if you can spot the common part in the sets of words below. Circle the common part.

A) 江　河　海　沙

B) 春　早　明　時/时

C) 吃　喝　叫　唱

D) 草/草　花/花　茶/茶　菜/菜

What do you notice about the words with similar components?

Answer:

A) All the words are related to water. B) All words are related to time. C) All words require a mouth. D) All those items are grown.

Mini Crosswords

Translate the clues into Chinese to fill in the crosswords.

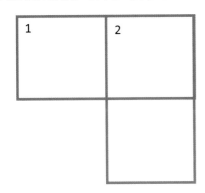

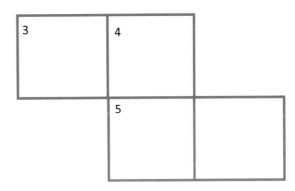

Across

1. Tomorrow

3. Worker

5. Saliva

Down

2. World

4. Population

Wordsearch

See if you can spot the Chinese words!

十	羊	玉	出	羊
出	十	二	月	毛
羊	王	出	玉	十
出	玉	羊	王	毛
名	十	名	十	子

1. 十二月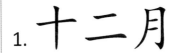

December

2. 出名

Famous

3. 王子

Prince

4. 羊毛

Wool

Colour!

We introduced you to some colours in our workbooks 1 and 2.

白○ 黑● 紅／红⬤ 黄／黄⬤

We will now introduce you how to write a new colour:

藍 蓝 **Blue**

Traditional Chinese Simplified Chinese laam4 lán

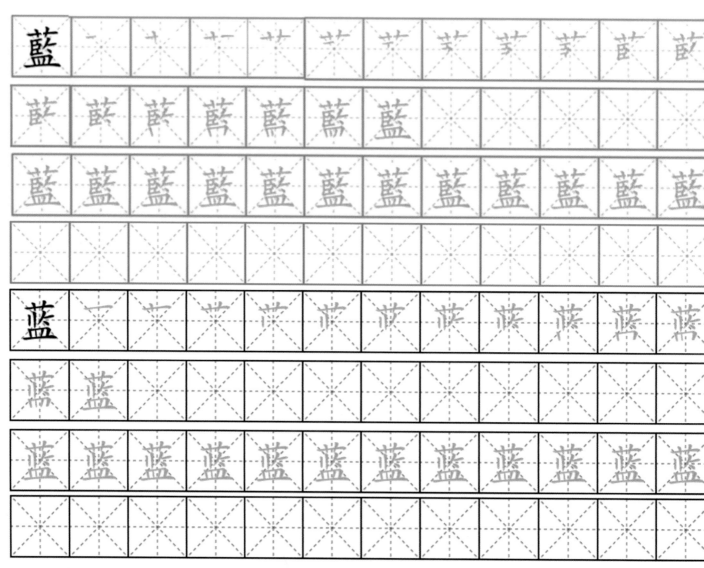

Colour the Flags!

Colour the flags with pens, pencils or crayons that match the spots.

Canada

紅／红⬤　白◯

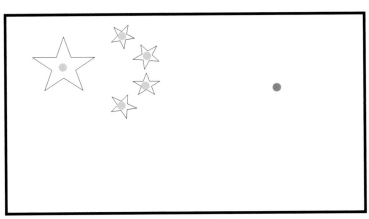

China

紅／红⬤

黃／黄◯

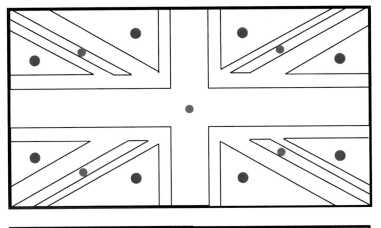

United Kingdom

紅／红⬤　白◯

藍／蓝⬤

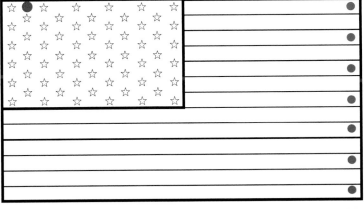

United States of America

紅／红⬤　白◯

藍／蓝⬤

Seasons

Match the Chinese word to the correct picture.

What is your favourite season? Draw your illustration below and label it.

Label It!

Label the various body parts below by picking a word from our word bank.

口　目　手　心　耳　牙　身　頭/头

Simplified Versus Traditional

Circle the Simplified Chinese word below.

a)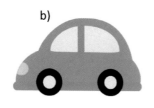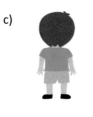
國 国

b)
車 车

c)
後 后

d)
學 学

e)
風 风

f)
門 门

g)
見 见

h)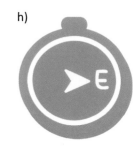
东 東

i)
熱 热

j)
關 关

k)
頭 头

l)
开 開

m)
時 时

n)
说 說

o)
問 问

p)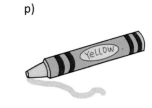
黃 黄

Monsters!

Finish these monster pictures by adding the Chinese word written underneath them!

口

手

身

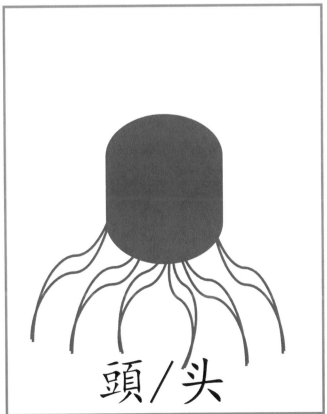

頭/头

Calendar

Match the month to the clues.

一月 ●   ● The start of a new year!

二月 ●   ● The last month of summer.

三月 ●   ● This month has 28 days usually but 29 in a leap year!

四月 ●   ● Beginning of Autumn!

五月 ●   ● Begins with A in English and has 30 days.

六月 ●   ● Americans typically celebrate Thanksgiving this month.

七月 ●   ● The month we carve pumpkins.

八月 ●   ● The start of Spring!

九月 ●   ● This month in English has just 3 letters.

十月 ●   ● This month has 30 days and begins with the letter J in English.

十一月 ●   ● The month before August.

十二月 ●   ● When Santa comes to visit!

Calculation Time

Do the maths below by filling in the blanks with numbers in Chinese.

虫

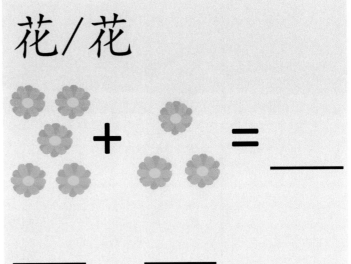

光

笑

车/车

白

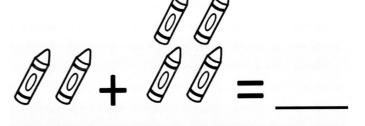

Label the Bar Chart

How many glasses of orange juice does everybody drink in a week?
Label the bar chart with numbers written in Chinese.

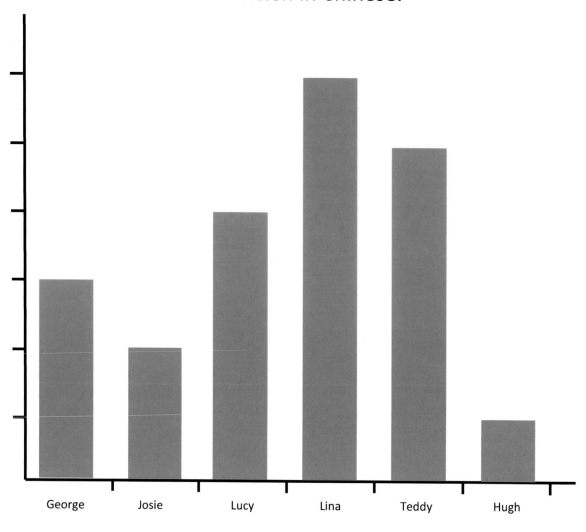

George Josie Lucy Lina Teddy Hugh

George

Josie

Lucy

Lina

Teddy

Hugh

Draw the Line

The words below are missing a stroke! Can you add in the missing stroke? Words in section A are missing a horizontal line. The first one has been done for you.

The words in this section are missing the vertical line. Please add them in. The first one has been done for you.

Opposites

Draw a line connecting the two opposite words. The first one has been done for you.

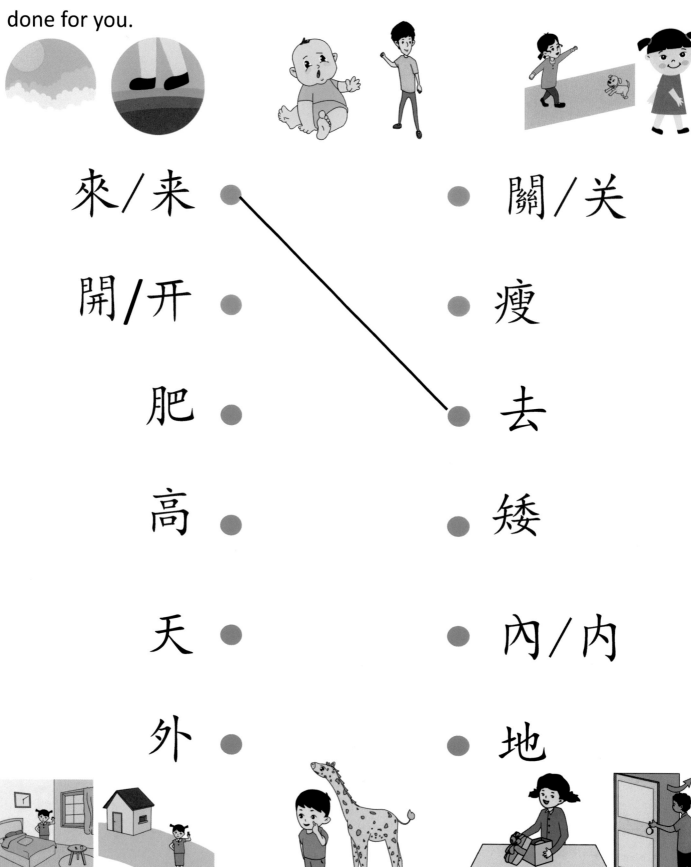

來 / 来   ●   ●   關 / 关

開 / 开   ●   ●   瘦

肥   ●   ●   去

高   ●   ●   矮

天   ●   ●   內 / 内

外   ●   ●   地

小 ●	● 下
白 ●	● 大
多 ●	● 右
上 ●	● 黑
左 ●	● 少
火 ●	● 水
男 ●	● 女

Fill in the Blank

Fill in the blank squares with a word from the word bank so that it matches the picture.

看　　快　　　家　　　　金

雪　　冷　　兒子　　女兒

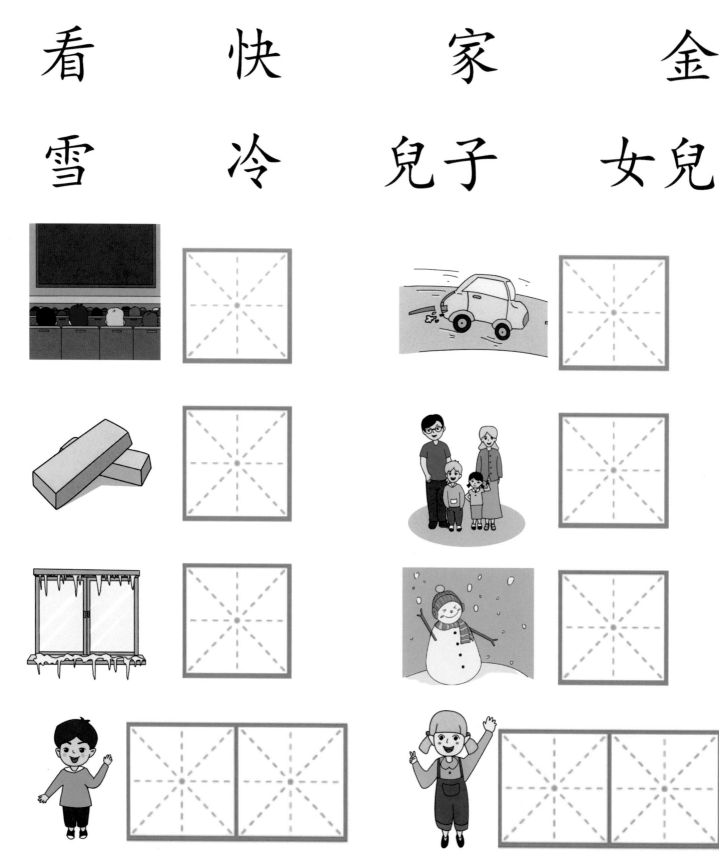

All About Directions

Match the Chinese word to the picture in each box then find the gold in the maze!

上 •   •

下 •   •

Start here

左 •   •

右 •   •

東/东 •   •

南 •   •

西 •   •

北 •   •

前 •   •

後/后 •   •

Match It

Draw a line matching the Chinese word to the correct picture.

方 ●

久 ●

半 ●

刀 ●

不 ●

名 ●

Which is Correct?

Chinese words can look similar. Circle the correct word to match the picture.

a)

肥　月

b)

友　又

c)

太　大

d)

石　有

e)

毛　老

f)

今　公

g)

雪　雨

h)

毛　手

i)

秋　火

Translator!

See if you can translate the sentences into Chinese by picking one word from each group below.

Group A

你 — You
我 — I/Me
她 — She/Her
他 — He/Him
哥哥 — Older Brother
弟弟 — Younger Brother

姐姐 — Older Sister
妹妹 — Younger Sister
爸爸 — Father
媽媽/妈妈 — Mother

Group B

學 — Learn
唱 — Sing
喝 — Drink
煮 — Cook
要 — Want
吃 — Eat
說/说 — Say/Speak

Group C

羊肉 — Lamb
牛肉 — Beef
魚/鱼 — Fish
雞/鸡 — Chicken

豬肉/猪肉 — Pork
水 — Water
中文 — Chinese
歌 — Song/Songs

a)

_____

You   drink   water

b)

_____

She   sings   songs

c)

_____

Father   cooks   beef

d)

_____

Mother   speaks   Chinese

Try some of your own sentences:

_____

_____

_____

Maths Time

Try to do the sums below.

a) 一 ＋ 四 ＝ ☐

b) 七 ＋ 六 － 九 ＝ ☐

c) 三 ＋ 五 ＋ 七 ＋ 八 ＝ ☐

Who's Who?

Label everybody in the picture.

媽媽/妈妈　爸爸　姐姐　妹妹　哥哥　弟弟

Certificate of Excellence

Congratulations!

_____ has successfully completed Chinese Writing Workbook 3.

SUPER SPEAK JUNIORS

Page 4
a) 一 b)三 c)五 d)二 e)四 f)六

Page 5
1 一， 2 二 ， 3 三， 4 四， 5 五， 6 六， 7 七， 8 八， 9 九， 10 十

Page 6
a) 人 b) 田 c) 米 d) 禾 e) 目 f)歌 g) 安 h)同 i) 王

Page 7
子 和 美 到 面 在

Page 10

Page 12
Bright 明, Early 早, Ancient 古, Minute/divide 分, Sing 唱, Male 男, Out 出

Page 13
Careful 小心, Kind 好心, Parents 父母, Chinese 中文, Tasty 可口, Morning 早上, Student 學生/学生, Birthday 生日, Volcano 火山, Understand 明白.

Page 14
A) 氵   B) 日   C) 口   D) 艹 艹

Page 15
1. 明天 2. 天下 3. 工人 4. 人口 5. 口水

十	羊	玉	出	羊
出	十	二	月	毛
羊	王	出	玉	十
出	玉	羊	王	毛
名	十	名	十	子

Page 17

Page 18

春 夏 秋 冬

Page 19

頭/头
耳
口
身
目
牙
心
手

Page 20
a)国 b)车 c)后 d)学 e)风 f)门 g)见 h)东 i)热 j)关 k)头 l)开 m)时 n)说 o)问 p)黄

Page 21
口mouth, 手 hand, 身 body, 頭/头 head.

Page 22

一月	The start of a new year!
二月	The last month of summer.
三月	This month has 28 days usually but 29 in a leap year!
四月	Beginning of Autumn!
五月	Begins with A in English and has 30 days.
六月	Americans typically celebrate Thanksgiving this month.
七月	The month we carve pumpkins.
八月	The start of Spring!
九月	This month in English has just 3 letters.
十月	This month has 30 days and begins with the letter J in English.
十一月	The month before August.
十二月	When Santa comes to visit!

Page 23

虫
~ + ~ = 六
二 四

花/花
+ = 八
五 三

光
+ = 七
二 六

车/车
+ = 十一
三 八

笑
+ = 十三
六 七

白
+ = 六
二 四

Page 24
1 一 Hugh, 2 二 Josie, 3 三 George, 4 四 Lucy, 5 五 Teddy, 6 六 Lina.

Page 25
好, 坐, 雨, 市, 文, 工, 間/间.

Page 26
來/来-去, 開-开/關-关, 肥-瘦, 高-矮, 天-地, 外-内.

Page 27
小-大, 白-黑, 多-少, 上-下, 左-右, 火-水, 男-女.

Page 28

看 快 家 金 雪 冷 兒子 女兒

Page 29

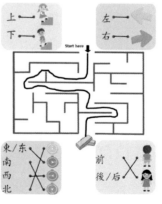

Page 30

方 久 半 刀 不 名

Page 31
a)肥 b)友 c)太 d)石 e)老 f)今 g)雪 h)手 i)秋

Page 33
a)你喝水　　b)她唱歌　　c)爸爸煮牛肉　　d)媽媽說中文/妈妈说中文
Page 34
a)五　　　b)四　　　c)二十三
Mother:媽媽/妈妈 Father: 爸爸 Older Sister: 姐姐 Younger sister: 妹妹 Older brother:哥哥 Younger brother:弟弟

Our Books

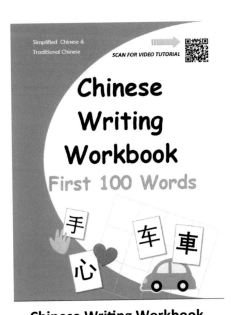

Chinese Writing Workbook
First 100 Words
Simplified & Traditional Chinese
with Pinyin & Jyutping

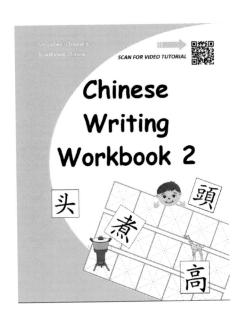

Chinese Writing Workbook 2
Simplified & Traditional Chinese
with Pinyin & Jyutping

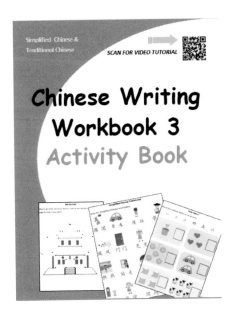

Chinese Writing Workbook 3
Simplified & Traditional Chinese
with Pinyin & Jyutping

Chinese Legends
Three Popular Stories
Bilingual Edition
English & Traditional Chinese
with Jyutping

Chinese Legends
Three Popular Stories
Bilingual Edition
English & Simplified Chinese
with Pinyin

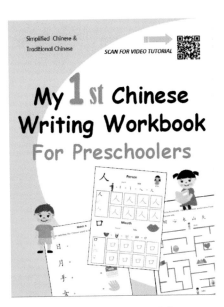

My 1st Chinese Writing
Workbook - Preschoolers
Simplified & Traditional
Chinese
with Pinyin & Jyutping

Words introduced in Workbook 1—First 100 Words

Scan the QR code or go to www.superspeakjuniors.com for the video tutorial on how to write and pronounce the words below in Chinese.

English	Traditional Chinese	Simplified Chinese
One	一	一
Two	二	二
Three	三	三
Four	四	四
Five	五	五
Six	六	六
Seven	七	七
Eight	八	八
Nine	九	九
Ten	十	十
Person	人	人
Child	子	子
Knife	刀	刀
Force	力	力
Also	又	又
Up	上	上
Down	下	下
Little	小	小
Big	大	大
Mouth	口	口
Mountain	山	山
Soil	土	土

English	Traditional Chinese	Simplified Chinese
Work	工	工
King	王	王
Sky	天	天
Water	水	水
Fire	火	火
Wood	木	木
Wheat	禾	禾
Do Not	不	不
Day	日	日
White	白	白
Eye	目	目
Month	月	月
Bright	明	明
Field	田	田
Living /Grow	生	生
Centre	中	中
Writing	文	文
Heart	心	心
Female	女	女
Male	男	男
Mother	母	母
Father	父	父

English	Traditional Chinese	Simplified Chinese
Cow	牛	牛
Sheep	羊	羊
Tooth/Teeth	牙	牙
Ears	耳	耳
Hand/Hands	手	手
Fur	毛	毛
Friends	友	友
Go	去	去
Out	出	出
Can	可	可
Stone	石	石
Left	左	左
Right	右	右
In	在	在
City	市	市
Year	年	年
Called	叫	叫
Name	名	名
Eat	吃	吃
Insect	虫	虫
Old	老	老
Have	有	有
Uncooked Rice	米	米
Light	光	光
Less	少	少
More	多	多
Early	早	早
Body	身	身

English	Traditional Chinese	Simplified Chinese
Sand	沙	沙
With	和	和
Laugh/Smile	笑	笑
Ground	地	地
Sit	坐	坐
Spring	春	春
Summer	夏	夏
Autumn	秋	秋
Winter	冬	冬
Rain	雨	雨
Fruit	果	果
Me/I	我	我
You	你	你
Good	好	好
She	她	她
He	他	他
Front	前	前
North	北	北
South	南	南
West	西	西
East	東	东
See	見	见
Door	門	门
Wind	風	风
Horse	馬	马
Car	車	车
Back	後	后
Learn	學	学

Words introduced in Chinese Writing Workbook 2

Scan the QR code or go to www.superspeakjuniors.com for the video tutorial on how to write and pronounce the words below in Chinese.

English	Traditional Chinese	Simplified Chinese
January	一月	一月
February	二月	二月
March	三月	三月
April	四月	四月
May	五月	五月
June	六月	六月
July	七月	七月
August	八月	八月
September	九月	九月
October	十月	十月
November	十一月	十一月
December	十二月	十二月
Population	人口	人口
Worker	工人	工人
Saliva	口水	口水
Tasty	可口	可口
Volcano	火山	火山
Birthday	生日	生日
Famous	出名	出名
Prince	王子	王子
Tomorrow	明天	明天
Understand	明白	明白

English	Traditional Chinese	Simplified Chinese
Wool	羊毛	羊毛
Careful	小心	小心
Kind	好心	好心
Chinese	中文	中文
Parents	父母	父母
Morning	早上	早上
The world	天下	天下
Student	學生	学生
Too	太	太
Square	方	方
Now/Today	今	今
Public	公	公
Ancient	古	古
Long	久	久
Jade	玉	玉
Minute/divide	分	分
Meat	肉	肉
Beef	牛肉	牛肉
Lamb	羊肉	羊肉
Safe	安	安
Half	半	半
Use	用	用

English	Traditional Chinese	Simplified Chinese
With	同	同
Inside	內	内
Outside	外	外
Beautiful	美	美
River	江	江
River	河	河
Sea	海	海
Arrive	到	到
Surface	面	面
Sing	唱	唱
Song	歌	歌
Drink	喝	喝
Cook	煮	煮
Look at	看	看
Want	要	要
Fast	快	快
Fat	肥	肥
Thin	瘦	瘦
Short	矮	矮
Tall	高	高
Family	家	家
Dog	狗	狗
Gold	金	金
Black	黑	黑
Snow	雪	雪
Cold	冷	冷
Older brother	哥哥	哥哥
Younger brother	弟弟	弟弟

English	Traditional Chinese	Simplified Chinese
Older sister	姐姐	姐姐
Younger sister	妹妹	妹妹
Father	爸爸	爸爸
Mother	媽媽	妈妈
Child	兒	儿
Son	兒子	儿子
Daughter	女兒	女儿
Grass	草	草
Flower	花	花
Tea	茶	茶
Fish	魚	鱼
Vegetables	菜	菜
Cat	貓	猫
Pig	豬	猪
Chicken	雞	鸡
Red	紅	红
Cloud	雲	云
Come	來	来
Room	間	间
Country	國	国
Ask	問	问
Says/said	說	说
Time	時	时
Head	頭	头
Close	關	关
Open	開	开
Hot	熱	热
Yellow	黃	黄

Made in the USA
Las Vegas, NV
07 November 2021

33936782R00026